Learn Danish in 500 Words

Learn Danish in 500 Words

Your Danish Learning Guide for a Quick Introduction to the Top 500 Words in Danish

by

Daniel Maluszczak

Noovy Publishing

2. Edition, 2023

Noovy Publishing

Table of Contents

1. Why you should learn Danish and why I started learning Danish

Hello, future Danish learner! With this Danish learning guide, you will be able to learn your first 500 Danish words easily and in a structured way. I understand that starting to learn a new language can be challenging and sometimes overwhelming, which is why this guide will focus only on the first 500 words. Once you've mastered those, you'll have a strong foundation of words upon which to build and further improve your Danish skills.

When I first started learning Danish, the only word I knew was "øl," which means beer. And similar to Germany, where I was born, beer is a significant part of Danish culture; you'll find Carlsberg and Tuborg in almost every bar.

By the way, you've just learned your first Danish word: "øl." Let's label this as Word #1.

I'm sure you have your personal reasons for wanting to learn Danish, but here are a few more reasons that might further motivate you:

First of all, Danish isn't that difficult if you already know English. Given their shared Germanic origins, the two languages have many similar words, and even the grammar is quite similar.

Second, Danish, Swedish, and Norwegian share many similarities because they all stem from the Old Norse language spoken by the Vikings. Therefore, with a solid grasp of Danish, you should be able to understand Swedish and Norwegian speakers easily and even learn those languages with relatively little extra effort.

There are also several practical benefits to learning Danish. If you decide to move to Denmark and want a job there, it's still beneficial to speak Danish even though most Danes are fluent in English. It can help you connect with and befriend more Danes. If you truly fall in love with Denmark and want to become a citizen, you'll need to achieve at least a B2 level in Danish to pass the citizenship test.

However, learning a new language is not just about practicality—it's about experiencing the beauty of another culture and opening your mind to a new way of thinking. So stay motivated and enjoy your journey!

Here's a quick word regarding the methodology we employ to facilitate learning of the initial 500 words. This guide primarily focuses on teaching you Danish vocabulary; therefore, there will be no emphasis on grammar, pronunciation, or specific language rules. However, there will occasionally be brief explanations about exceptions to help you identify them when, for example, reading a simple text. This is to prevent confusion when encountering these forms for the first time, but please note, the level of detail in these explanations will be moderate.

Moreover, the chapters will be arranged by topics, with each chapter containing a set of vocabulary that you can learn in a structured manner as they are presented in groups of ten. We'll cover the basics until chapter nine; beyond that, you're free to alter the chapter sequence if you wish to prioritize certain topics and learn them earlier.

Without further ado, let's begin by examining the three extra letters the Danes incorporate into their words by exploring the Danish Alphabet.

2. The Danish Alphabet

Compared to the English alphabet, the Danish one includes some special characters that we should examine before delving into the first words we aim to learn. Interestingly, the official name of the Danish alphabet is the "Danish and Norwegian alphabet," because, as you might have already surmised, the Danes and Norwegians share an alphabet. This 29-letter variant of the Latin alphabet was adopted by Denmark as recently as 1948 (and by Norway in 1917), and it incorporates all 26 English letters plus three additional ones. It was only in 1980 that **W** and **V** were recognized as separate letters in Danish. Prior to that, **W** was simply a variation of **V**, so older versions of the Danish alphabet song still mention 28 letters.

Below, you'll find the entire alphabet, but our primary focus will be on the last three letters.

#	Letter		Phonetic	#	Letter		Phonetic
1	A	a	[ɛʔ]	16	P	p	[pʰe̡ʔ]
2	B	b	[pe̡ʔ]	17	Q	q	[kʰuʔ]
3	C	c	[se̡ʔ]	18	R	r	[ɛɐ̯]
4	D	d	[te̡ʔ]	19	S	s	[es]
5	E	e	[e̡ʔ]	20	T	t	[tsʰe̡ʔ]
6	F	f	[ef]	21	U	u	[uʔ]
7	G	g	[ke̡ʔ]	22	V	v	[ve̡ʔ]
8	H	h	[hɔʔ]	23	W	w	[tʌpəlve̡ʔ]
9	I	i	[iʔ]	24	X	x	[eks]
10	J	j	[jʌð]	25	Y	y	[yʔ]
11	K	k	[kʰɔʔ]	26	Z	z	[set]
12	L	l	[el]	27	Æ	æ	[eʔ]
13	M	m	[em]	28	Ø	ø	[øʔ]
14	N	n	[en]	29	Å	å	[ɔʔ]
15	O	o	[oʔ]				

The extra letters you should care about are **Æ, Ø** and **Å**.

3. Get to know some basic pronouns

Let's begin with some of the pronouns found in the Danish language. Interestingly, they are quite similar to those in English, with the same structure of pronouns used. Below in the table, you'll find a list of the ones you should prioritize learning.

#	Danish	English
2	jeg	I
3	du	you
4	han	he
5	hun	she
6	den/det*	it
7	vi	we
8	de	they
9	i	you (plural)

As mentioned in the introduction, our current aim is to grasp only the basics of vocabulary, bypassing grammar and rules. However, when reading elementary Danish texts, it might be helpful to understand some basic anomalies in vocabulary to prevent confusion. Even within the pronouns, there's an unusual form that occasionally occurs in Danish.

The neutral pronoun "it" has two forms in Danish: "**den**" and "**det**". They are used depending on the noun they're replacing. If they replace a word that ends with "-et," you should use "**det**." For words ending with "-en," it's "**den**"

Having acquainted ourselves with the initial eight pronouns, let's move on to the basic possessive pronouns. They indicate ownership and will prove useful in basic conversations.

#	Danish	English
10	min*	my
11	din**	your
12	hans	his
13	hendes	hers
14	dens/dets***	its
15	vores	our
16	jeres	your
17	deres	theirs

Again, there are some exceptions, but this time they apply to three of the pronouns.

Officially, there are three forms: "**min**", "**mit**," and "**mine**". "**Min**" and "**mit**" are used for singular forms, while "**mine**" is used for the plural. For now, it might be easier to ignore the difference between "**min**" and "**mit**".

** The word "your" when addressing a single person, also has three forms: "**din**" "**dit**" and "**dine**" with "**din**" and "**dit**" indicating singular and "**dine**" the plural form.

*** Similarly, as with vocabulary #6, "**dens**" and "**dets**" are used depending on the ending of the word being replaced.

From this point forward, I plan to provide vocabulary in sets of ten to simplify your learning process. Since the number of pronouns in the Danish language doesn't total ten, you'll find three additional words at the end of this chapter. These words are useful for connecting words or sentences and will prove beneficial later. You can expect to see them in every text you read.

#	Danish	English
18	og	and
19	eller	or
20	men	but

4. Some basic verbs

Being able to tell the things that you are doing or other entities are doing is important in your first attempts to form a full sentence. Again we focus on the important verbs and most common forms, while ignoring the specifics of grammar and special forms.

#	Danish	English
21	være	be
22	gå	go
23	har	have
24	kan	can
25	vil have	want
26	sætte	put
27	skal	must
28	brug	need
29	skulle	should
30	sige	say

Below on this page you will find a table with some exemplary conjugations of the verb, some regular and some irregular.

Danish	English	Danish infinitive
jeg er	I am	være
jeg har	I have	har
jeg siger	I say	sige
du laver	You make	lave
vi vil have	We have	Vil have
Du kan	you can	kan

As you may have already guessed the regular conjugation adds an -r at the end of the verb, while irregular ones can look completely different. Luckily the irregular form is the same for a lot of verbs, so the conjugation of *be* (#21 **være**) would look like this:

Danish	English
jeg er	I am
du er	you are
han er	he is
vi er	we are
de er	they are

After knowing a bit too much about the conjugations of verbs let us add another ten to the list with the table below.

#	Danish	English
31	at rejse	to travel
32	at komme	to come
33	at blive kaldt	to be called
34	at give	to give
35	at lave/gøre	to make/do
36	at se	to see
37	at cykle	to bike
38	at løbe	to run
39	at tale	to speak
40	at snakke	to talk

Here are some examples:

Jeg rejser	I travel
Du løber	You run
Vi snakker	We talk

5. Some basic but useful nouns

We should not wait too long to learn the first nouns, because they are often the most essential part to understand context and knowing some of the most common ones can help you understand basic things. And better get ready to learn many more nouns, because they are by far the most common vocabulary you will learn in this guide. So let us start with ten basic but important nouns.

#	Danish	English
41	mad	food
42	vand	water
43	hjem	home
44	dag	day
45	nat	night
46	politi	police
47	bil	car
48	vej	road
49	person	person
50	telefon	phone

From the English language we already know that nouns come with an article, and the concept is similar in Danish. Luckily there is only one article that is used for all nouns, unlike in other languages like French or German where there are two or even three articles depending on whether the noun is female, male or neutral.

But coming back to Danish there is only one, in the table below the article and related words that indicate amounts are summarized.

#	Danish	English
51	den	the
52	en/et	a
53	en	one
54	nogle	some
55	få	few
56	alle	all
57	ingen	none

The car would be **den bil** and *a phone* would be **en telefon**

Now with the basic components of a sentence at hand we are able to form some very basic sentences. It is not the longest sentence, but still a good start. Fortunately, basic Danish sentences have the same structure as English ones, so let us take a look at some super basic sentences you are able to form now in the table on the next page.

Eamples of basic Danish sentences:

Danish	English
jeg har en bil	I have a car
det er nat	it is night
jeg vil have mad	I want food
jeg har ingen telefon	I have no phone

We add three new words to be able to say *"I learn Danish and it is fun!"*

#	Danish	English
58	lærer	learn
59	dansk	Danish
60	sjovt	fun

In Danish this would be: ***Jeg lærer dansk, og det er sjovt!***

Before moving to learn more nouns, we should take a quick look on some common adjectives that will be helpful and reoccurring while using Danish in the next chapter.

6. Common adjectives

To describe how things are and especially to give some context to our nouns we will learn some basic adjectives. We will go with the top 20 first and add more later for each category.

#	Danish	English
61	stor	big
62	lille	small
63	hurtig	fast
64	langsom	slow
65	lyse	bright
66	mørk	dark
67	blød	soft
68	hård	hard
69	billig	cheap
70	dyrt	expensive

#	Danish	English
71	dårligt	bad
72	godt	good
73	ren	clean
74	snavset	dirty
75	tom	empty
76	fuld	full
77	støjende	noisy
78	stille	quiet
79	unge	young
80	gamle	old

Below you see some example sentences with those adjectives. Note that the order of the words in a sentence might be different from English, but this will in most cases not pose any serious problems for understanding simple texts.

Jeg har an hurtig bil	I have a fast car
Det er en stille nat	It is a quiet night
Han er et ungt menneske	He is a young person

7. Asking questions

Being able to ask questions is an important part of communication, so here is a quick overview of all the important interrogative pronouns you can use to ask questions.

#	Danish	English
81	hvor?	Where?
82	hvem?	Who?
83	hvordan?	How?
84	hvad?	What?
85	hvorfor?	Why?

And here are some examples how you can use those to ask basic questions:

Hvad er dit navn?	What is your name?
Hvad er klokken?	What is the time?
Hvor er bilen?	Where is the car?
Hvorfor løber du?	Why are you running?

To answer the question about where something is located, you can use the following words to describe the relative position of an object or person.

#	Danish	English
86	under	under
87	over	over
88	venstre	left
89	højre	right
90	bag	behind

And here are some examples how you can use those prepositions:

Hvad er der under sengen?	What is under the bed?
Drej til højre	Turn right
Hvad er der bag døren?	What is behind the door?
Hans venstre arm	His left arm

Find even more prepositions of place on the graphic next page.

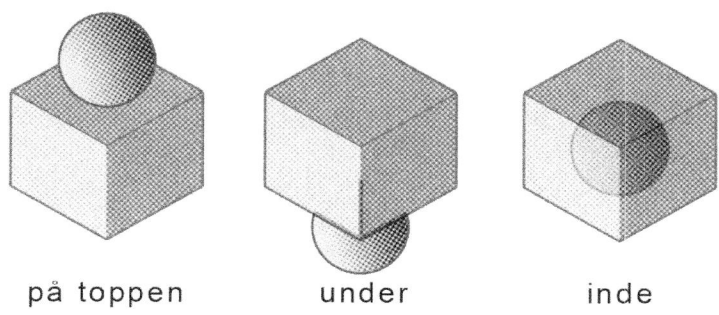

på toppen   under   inde

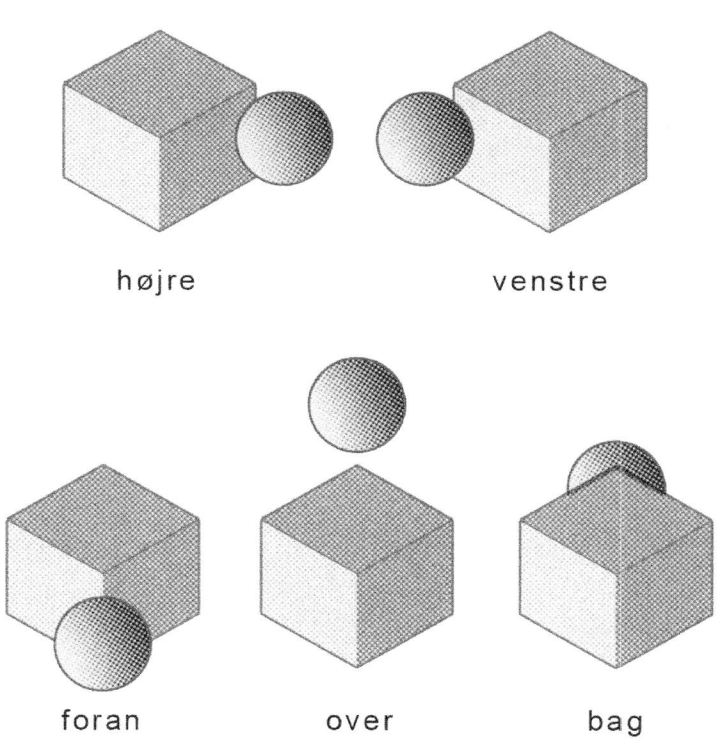

højre   venstre

foran   over   bag

8. Talk about things you can do

weahter you are just walking around, learning Danish or jut sleeping, those are all activities you can do. Some more active than others, but still activities.

Below find a list with the 20 most common ones you might encounter.

#	Danish	English
91	stå	stand
92	gå	walk
93	vandretur	hike
94	søvn	sleep
95	se tv	watch TV
96	spil	play
97	svømme	swim
98	parti	party
99	skrive	write
100	arbejde	work

Whooo, milestone of 100 words reached!

#	Danish	English
101	møde	meet
102	forberede	prepare
103	lære	learn
104	dans	dance
105	sidde	sit
106	slap af	relax
107	klatre	climb
108	læs	read
109	vask	wash
110	drikke	drink

And here are some examples:

Jeg vasker mine hænder	I wash my hands
Jeg læser en bog	I read a book
Jeg lærer dansk	I learn Danish

9. Eating out

After learning about some activities in the chapter before, now let us take a close look at another activity: Eating out in a restaurant or diner.

If you have been to Denmark before you will have noticed how expensive everything is here and especially eating out is much more expensive here than in other European nations. Nevertheless, you will probably encounter situations where you will want to order some food or dine in a restaurant.

#	Danish	English
111	restaurant	restaurant
112	at bestille	to order
113	tag væk	takeaway
114	fastfood	fast-food
115	spisekort	menu
116	flaske	bottle
117	at betale	to pay
118	med kontanter	by cash
119	med kort	by card
120	at spise	to eat

And in case you want to order something specific or just the vegetarian variant of a dish, here are the words to use.

#	Danish	English
121	pommes frites	fries
122	kaffe	coffee
123	te	tea
124	vin	wine
125	suppe	soup
126	salt	salt
127	peber	pepper
128	krydret	spicy
129	vegetarisk	vegetarian
130	vegansk	vegan

And remember the words you already know #41 **mad** and #42 **vand**

And here are some examples:

Jeg drikker te	I drink tea
Har du vegetarisk mad?	Do you have vegetarian food?

10. How to greet in Danish

Did you realize that we still did not talk about the basics on how to greet people and tell them your name? Well one reason for this is that in most cases people will understand you when you say *hi* (and vocabulary #131 shows why) and tell them your name in Denmark. But for a bit more complex situations we will now cover the greetings and introductions in Danish.

#	Danish	English
131	hej	hello/hi
132	god morgen	good morning
133	god aften	good evening
134	god eftermiddag	good afternoon
135	godnat	good night
136	navn	name
137	fornavn	first name
138	efternavn	last name
139	hvor gammel	how old
140	bor	To live

Again some examples how you can use the words

Hej mit navn er...	Hello, my name is...
Jeg bor i Aalborg	I live in Aalborg
Jeg er 25 år gammel	I am 25 years old

11. At the municipal office

You arrive in Denmark and now have to deal with the municipality or need to organize some official stuff, here is some basic vocabulary for this case. Even though the Danish bureaucratic system is very efficient and many things can be organised online, it sometimes is still necessary to book in-person appointments, for example for the registration of a CPR number. The CPR number in Denmark, is a personal identification number similar to a social security number but covers for far more functions and is needed for all things related to the government and often also financial services.

#	Danish	English
141	dokument	document
142	brev	letter
143	underskrift	signature
144	frimærke	stamp
145	forsegle	seal
146	ansøgning	application
147	kontrakt	contract
148	id-kort	ID-card
149	kuvert	envelope
150	kontor	office

12. At the hospital

Let us hope you will never need it, but sometimes it is unavoidable to see a doctor. If that is the case you will find the most important words here.

Did you know that Danish health care system is one of the best ones in the world? If you get a yellow health card because you study or work here you can get necessary medical services for free, dental care is not included though.

#	Danish	English
151	læge	doctor
152	hospital	hospital
153	smerte	pain
154	brækket	broken
155	pille	pill
156	recept	prescription
157	ambulance	ambulance
158	desinfektionsmiddel	disinfectant
159	brække sig	puke
160	sprøjte	syringe

In case you need to tell the doctor about your specific condition here are the ten of the most common ones. If you are in an emergency situation you should call (+45) 112 for police, fire department or ambulance services in Denmark. The phone number (+45) 1813 can be used to directly speak to medical staff to get first aid for injuries or a sudden illness. Before going to Denmark you should look up the up-to-date emergency numbers. Just in case.

#	Danish	English
161	hoste	cough
162	ondt i halsen	sore throat
163	hovedpine	headache
164	mavepine	stomachache
165	kvalme	nausea
166	forkølelse	common cold
167	trukket muskel	pulled muscle
168	højt blodtryk	high blood pressure
169	Diabetes	Diabetes
170	allergi	allergy

To wish somebody to get better soon you can say: **God bedring**

13. Body parts

Plus it is also useful to not only be able to tell what kind of emergency one has, but also to be able to tell what body part is affected. So here you find ten body parts that you probably also have.

#	Danish	English
171	hoved	head
172	øje	eye
173	arm	arm
174	hånd	hand
175	finger	finger
176	ben	leg
177	fod	foot
178	mund	mouth
179	bug	belly
180	balder	buttocks

14. Travelling to Denmark: Airport

Welcome to Denmark! Or if you are returning: welcome back. If you decided not to go by train or by car, one of the remaining ways to enter Denmark is by plane. Since Denmark is a comparably small country, you will probably not board many domestic flights, but arriving here from abroad is still a possibility, and yeah I know almost every sign at any airport around the world also offers an English translation and most of the staff is also English speaking, but it is still nice to know at least some words, you never know in what other contexts you might need them...

#	Danish	English
181	lufthavn	airport
182	flyvemaskine	plane
183	afgang	departure
184	ankomst	arrival
185	fly	flight
186	vindue sæde	window seat
187	gang sæde	aisle seat
188	midterste sæde	middle seat
189	sikkerhedssele	seatbelt
190	sikkerhedskontrol	security check

And another ten words you might need before check-in:

#	Danish	English
191	håndbagage	carry-on baggage
192	bagage	luggage
193	check-in	check-in
194	boardingkort	boarding-pass
195	skranken	counter
196	at gå ombord	to board
197	port	gate
198	at reservere	to book
199	rundtur	round trip
200	en-vejs tur	one-way trip

Here are some example sentences:

Jeg har et gangsæde	I have an aisle seat
Jeg reserverede et fly til Aalborg	I booked a flight to Aalborg
Afgang til København fra gate 2	Departure to Copenhagen from gate 2

Getting to and from the airport is often done via public transportation, so here are some useful words for this case. For you to know, public transport like buses and trains are often very expensive and locals often make use of the good biking infrastructure in cities. At the time of writing a single use, one-way bus ticket in Aalborg is around 24 kr. that is about 3.20€ or $3.25.

#	Danish	English
201	bus	bus
202	tog	train
203	taxa	taxi
204	sikkerhedssele	seat belt
205	billet	ticket
206	busstoppested	bus stop
207	hovedbanegården	central station
208	næste stop	next stop
209	chauffør	driver
210	tidsplan	timetable

#	Danish	English
211	at rejse	to travel
212	sent	late
213	en gang	on time
214	billetkontrollør	ticket inspector
215	gyldig billet	valid ticket
216	endelige destination	final destination
217	reservation	reservation
218	busstoppested	bus stop
219	skifte	transfer/change
220	udgang	exit

And here are some examples on how to use them:

Jeg rejser med bus	I am travelling by bus
Mit tog er forsinket	My train is late
Vi reserverede en taxa	We reserved a taxi

15. At the store

Let us do some groceries and learn some helpful words you can use while in the store. The trend of organic foods and a vegetarian or even vegan lifestyle is very popular in Denmark, so expect many of these products in supermarket shelves. Compared to conventional products they are more expensive and watch out, many times they try to simulate the taste and look of certain products, and you will mostly only find out by tasting them or translating the labels into English before buying.

#	Danish	English
221	dagligvarer	groceries
222	butik	store
223	parkeringsplads	parking lot
224	Indkøbskurv	shopping cart
225	indkøbsliste	shopping list
226	kvittering	receipt
227	pose	bag
228	kurv	basket
229	engros	wholesale
230	økologisk	organic

When buying you should also be able to know what is cheap and what is expensive in Denmark. When coming from abroad to Denmark in most cases prices will be much higher compared to other countries, this is not only because on average the pay of employees is higher, but also because there is for example a very high VAT rate of about 25% for most products.

#	Danish	English
231	salg	sale
232	billig	cheap
233	dyr	expensive
234	købe	buy
235	kasseapparat	cash register
236	pris	price
237	supermarked	supermarket
238	discounter	discounter
239	minimarked	mini-mart
240	merværdiafgift	VAT

And here are some examples on how to use them:

Brødet er til salg	The bread is on sale
Discounts har billige priser	Discounters have cheap prices

16. At the store: things you can buy

Now that you can articulate about basic grocery shopping we should take a look at the broad categories you can shop and later even go further into detail with some useful products you can purchase in the supermarket or discounter of your choice.

#	Danish	English
241	mejeriprodukter	dairy products
242	kød	meat
243	skaldyr	seafood
244	frugter	fruits
245	grøntsager	vegetables
246	Instant måltid	instant meal
247	opbakning	backing
248	apotek	drugstore
249	husholdningsprodukter	household products
250	toiletartikler	toiletries

Denmark along with some other northern and western European countries is a front-runner in sustainable packaging. You will find many products packed in easily recyclable and sustainable wrapping, but also a packaging deposit system for bottles and cans, where you pay an extra deposit for the container that is then returned when you bring back the bottle or can to the store. So do not forget to bring back your empty plastic bottles or **øl**-cans.

#	Danish	English
251	krukke	jar
252	kan	can
253	flaske	bottle
254	net	net
255	kold	cold
256	frossen	frozen
257	pakke	package
258	beholder	container
259	løs	loose
260	frisk	fresh

And here are some examples on how to use them:

En kold flaske øl	A cold bottle of beer
Et net af appelsiner	A net of oranges

Let us say you are in the store and are looking for specific products, the list below will give you the vocabulary for the most common things you could need from the food department.

#	Danish	English
261	pasta	pasta
262	nudler	noodles
263	mel	flour
264	sukker	sugar
265	salt	salt
266	krydderier	spices
267	juice	juice
268	fisk	fish
269	olie	oil
270	smør	butter

And here are some examples on how to use them:

Har du frossen fisk?	Do you have frozen fish?
Jeg skal bruge en flaske olie	I need a bottle of oil

And here are some more words you can put on your **indkøbsliste** (#155)

#	Danish	English
271	brød	bread
272	marmelade	jam
273	yoghurt	yoghurt
274	mælk	milk
275	søde sager	sweets
276	dessert	dessert
277	korn	cereals
278	ris	rice
279	sovs	sauce
280	ost	cheese

17. Units, Measures and more

When doing your groceries or when cooking, you should know some basic units, so you know what you are working with.

If you are used to the metric system congratulations, because Denmark uses the metric system and the names for the different types of units are quite similar to the English ones.

#	Danish	English
281	meter	Meter
282	gram	Gram
283	liter	Liter
284	grader celsius	degree celsius
285	Kilo-	Kilo-
286	Milli-	Milli-
287	Centi-	Centi-
288	længde	length
289	vægt	weight
290	volumen	volume

And just a small fun fact I found out during my research: originally **en meter** (#281) was defined as one divided by ten million of the distance between the North Pole and the Equator, and the measurement had to go through Paris, where the Metric system was introduced back then to standardize all units across the country. Today this definition of a Meter is not valid anymore, instead it is defined as the distance that light travels in a second multiplied by 1/299,792,458 for all those math and physics interested number fanatics out there. Denmark introduced the metric system in 1907, after using its own unit system, the Danish Mile and the Danish Pound, for over 200 years.

And here are some additional translations for commonly used words connected with the units.

#	Danish	English
291	temperatur	temperature
292	hastighed	speed
293	svær	heavy
294	let	light
295	hurtig	fast
296	langsom	slow
297	varmt	hot
298	at koge	to boil
299	stor	big
300	lille	small

And here are some examples on how to use them:

Han har en hurtig bil	He has a fast car
Maden er varm	The food is hot

18. How to count

In chapter **tretten** (#314) we take a look at the numbers in Danish and how to count. First the single digit numbers:

#	Danish	English
301	nul	zero
302	en	one
303	to	two
304	tre	three
305	fire	four
306	fem	five
307	seks	six
308	syv	seven
309	otte	eight
310	ni	nine

Starting from 13 the numbers are combined the same way we do in the English language, but be caution, the names for 14, 17 and 18 deviate quite a lot from the expected form and should be memorised separately.

#	Danish	English
311	ti	ten
312	elleve	eleven
313	tolv	twelve
314	tretten	13
315	fjorten	14
316	femten	15
317	seksten	16
318	sytten	17
319	atten	18
320	nitten	19

Starting from twenty, counting follows this structure:

Second digit + og (#18) + first digit.

Everything would be written with no spaces in between. So 21 would be **enogtyve** ("one and twenty" literally translated) see all the numbers from 20 to 29 below.

20	tyve	25	femogtyve
21	enogtyve	26	seksogtyve
22	toogtyve	27	syvogtyve
23	treogtyve	28	otteogtyve
24	fireogtyve	29	niogtyve

Unfortunately counting on further gets somewhat confusing in Danish because the decadic numbers do not follow the same pattern as in English. Instead there is some other logic to count, but learning the words just by heart is easier for now.

#	Danish	English
321	tyve	20
322	tredive	30
323	fyrre	40
324	halvtreds	50
325	tres	60
326	halvfjerds	70
327	firs	80
328	halvfems	90
329	hundrede	100
330	tohundrede	200

Taking a look at for example 60 and 80, we see that the names are similar to the danish three (tre #304) and four (fire #305), this is no coincidence and there is some logic behind it. Those numbers are counted in steps of twenty, so taking three times 20 would result in 60 and taking four times 20 results in 80. Taking this now to the next level with 50, 70 and 90 we see that the name suggest "half threes" for 50, here the logic is that the number contains again three times twenty, but the last 20 is only a half, so ten. Counting this up results in 50 (20 + 20 + ½ 20 = 50). The same holds for 70 and 90.

And even more numbers, the pattern should be the same counting even further on.

#	Danish	English
331	tusind	1000
332	totusinde	2000
333	titusinde	10 000
334	tyve tusind	20 000
335	hundrede tusinde	100 000
336	to hundrede tusinde	200 000
337	million	1 000 000
338	to millioner	2 000 000
339	halv	half
340	kvart	quarter

And here are some extra words in case you need to do some calculations.

Danish	English
tilføje	add (+)
trække fra	subtract (-)
gange	multiply (x)
dividere	divide (/)

19. Marty, the time machine worked! Can you tell me the time, the date and the year?

Even if the laws of physics we know do not allow for time travel like in the *Back to the Future* movies, it is useful to know how to tell the time and the date in Danish, maybe a danish time traveler from a parallel universe might ask you about it some day...

Even though in such a case the first question probably would be about the year, we start with the weeks and the months.

#	Danish	English
341	uge	week
342	dag	day
343	mandag	Monday
344	tirsdag	Tuesday
345	onsdag	Wednesday
346	torsdag	Thursday
347	fredag	Friday
348	lørdag	Saturday
349	søndag	Sunday
350	weekend	weekend

And now the **tolv** (#313) months in one year.

#	Danish	English
351	Januar	January
352	Februar	February
353	Marts	March
354	April	April
355	Kan	May
356	Juni	June
357	Juli	July
358	August	August
359	September	September
360	Oktober	October
361	November	November
362	December	December
363	måned	month
364	år	year
365	årligt	annual
366	kvartalsvis	quarterly
367	månedlige	monthly
368	midtår	mid-year
369	fødselsdag	birthday
370	nytår	New years

20. Now tell me the time

In Denmark the 24-hour system is generally used to tell the time, though when telling the time orally the 12-hour system is also an option widely used and understood. Denmark lies within the Central European Time Zone (CET) that is one hour ahead of the UTC (Coordinated Universal Time), but switches to the Central European Summer Time (CEST) in summer which is two hours ahead of UTC - this practice is commonly referred to as Daylight Saving Time and is put in action to make better use of the daylight in the summer months by setting the clocks forward by one hour. In the fall months the clock is then set back by one hour. This practice is still in place at the time of writing this guide, but could soon be scrapped in the whole European Union after a vote to pursue a change in this system across the block in 2019. But now coming back to the vocabulary in this chapter:

#	Danish	English
371	tid	time
372	time	hour
373	minut	minute
374	sekund	second
375	ur	clock
376	sommertid	Daylight Saving Time
377	om morgenen	In the morning
378	om eftermiddagen	In the afternoon
379	midnat	midnight
380	middag	noon

Now let's tell the specific time, here are some examples, you can use the same pattern for the other times.

#	Danish	English
381	klokken er to	it is two o'clock
382	klokken er ti minutter i fire	it is ten minutes to four
383	klokken er kvart over et	it is quarter past one
384	klokken er halv ni*	it is half past eight
385	klokken er 30 minutter over otte	it is 30 minutes past eight
386	på et kvarter	in a quarter of an hour
387	på ti minutter	in ten minutes
388	sent	late
389	en gang	on time
390	tidlig	early

* instead of using the logic that it is half an hour into the full hour, in Danish one would say that the next hour is half an hour away. So instead of saying it is half past eight, one would say it is nine in half an hour, so you should count up the hour by one when using this phrase. In case this is confusing, just use the form of #385 to express the same time.

21. Home sweet home

Whether a rented apartment or your own house, you will probably have at least some of these rooms and now will be able to tell your friends what rooms you are talking about during that room tour you are giving them.

#	Danish	English
391	værelse	room
392	køkken	kitchen
393	badeværelse	bathroom
394	stue	living room
395	gang	Hallway
396	trappeopgang	stairwell
397	indgang	entry
398	dør	door
399	vindue	window
400	børneværelse	children's room

And now some basic stuff you might have in your home.

#	Danish	English
401	bord	table
402	stol	chair
403	television	TV
404	fjern	remote
405	skrivebord	desk
406	seng	bed
407	skab	cupboard
408	sofa	sofa
409	lampe	lamp
410	lys	light

And here are some examples on how to use them:

Stolen står i stuen	The chair is in the living room
Jeg tænder lyset i køkkenet	I turn on the light in the kitchen

22. In the Bathroom

After a good sleep the first thing many people do nowadays is taking a look at their phone, at least according to some studies. 30 years ago most people probably would have answered that the first thing they do is to go to the bathroom. Today many people probably also combine both activities in their morning routine, so let us take a look at some things in your bathroom and how they are called in Danish.

#	Danish	English
411	håndklæde	towel
412	sæbe	soap
413	shampoo	shampoo
414	at vaske	to wash
415	bruser	shower
416	håndvask	sink
417	bad	bath
418	tandpasta	toothpaste
419	tandbørste	tooth brush
420	toilet	toilet

23. In the kitchen

Besides cooking meals for the everyday hunger, meeting and cooking with friends is a common activity in Denmark. If you ever participate in such a gathering, you should know at least the basic vocabulary needed in the kitchen.

#	Danish	English
241	at bage	to bake
242	at klippe	to cut
243	at stege	to fry
244	at koge	to boil
245	at røre	to stir
246	at skrælle	to peel
247	pande	pan
248	gryde	pot
249	låg	lid
430	spatel	spatula

When serving the meal, you prepared before you can use this vocabulary to describe or ask for cutlery and dishes.

#	Danish	English
431	kniv	knife
432	gaffel	fork
433	ske	spoon
434	spiseskefuld	tablespoon
435	teskefuld	teaspoon
436	plade	plate
437	skål	bowl
438	glas	glass
439	kop	cup
440	strå	straw

And I hope that your kitchen is equipped with some of those things, otherwise eating out will be the only option you have.

#	Danish	English
441	køleskab	fridge
442	fryser	freezer
443	håndvask	sink
444	tryk	tap
445	mikroovn	microwave
446	brødrister	toaster
447	ovn	oven
448	komfur	stove
449	kvæg	cattle (water cooker*)
450	svamp	sponge

* in Denmark and other European countries it is common to have a water cooker, that allows for much more efficient water boiling.

24. Some fruits and vegetables

Denmark is a very healthy country and this is also reflected in the cuisine you find there. But before getting our hands on some recipes we take a look at some important and healthy ingredients. First some fruits.

#	Danish	English
451	æble	apple
452	banan	banana
453	citron	lemon
454	kirsebær	cherry
455	jordbær	strawberry
456	blåbær	blueberry
457	hindbær	raspberry
458	avocado	avocado
459	drue	grape
460	orange	orange

And for the healthy meal here some popular and important vegetables in the Danish cuisine, nothing exotic though.

#	Danish	English
461	kartoffel	potato
462	gulerod	carrot
463	broccoli	broccoli
464	paprika	paprika
465	løg	onion
466	hvidløg	garlic
467	gitter	lattice
468	tomat	tomato
469	champignon	mushroom
470	agurk	cucumber

25. More ingredients

And for the BBQ fans and everyone with a mixed diet, here are some common meat and fish types you find in Danish supermarkets.

#	Danish	English
471	bøf	beef
472	svinekød	pork
473	kylling	chicken
474	lam	lamb
475	hakket kød	minced meat
476	pølse	sausage
477	laks	salmon
478	reje	shrimp
479	hummer	lobster
480	østers	oyster

26. Æbleflæsk recipe

Get ready now to cook a traditional Danish dish called **Æbleflæsk**. The literal translation of this dish is *Apple Pork*, and it is mainly served for Christmas (**jul**) dinner. The tree main ingredients are **æble** (#451), thin **svinekød** (#472) strips and **løg** (#465).

Here is a list of the ingredients you need, the estimated time to prepare is about 20 minutes, but the actual working time is much less.

2	apples
1	onion
2 slices	streaky pork*
2 slices	rye bread
1 teaspoon	sugar
1 pinch	salt

*In case you do not have this type of pork at home, bacon will also do. If using bacon remember that it is already salty, so do not add any more salt, and you might need to add some extra oil or butter when cooking the onions and apples. The result will obviously taste differently, but is still a super tasty dish.

And here is how you prepare the dish:

1. Fry the pork in a pan for about 10 minutes, sprinkle with a bit of salt.

2. slice the onions into thin stripes.

3. peel and slice the apples into thin slices.

4. After the pork is done with a good brown color, take it out of the pan. Leave the grease inside the pan and add the onions.

5. When the onions start getting first brown spots add the apples and put a lid to close the pan.

6. Keep the onions and apples steaming for about 15-20 minutes on medium heat and keep them stirring. Add some sugar after 10 minutes.

7. Prepare the rye bread, add the stripes of pork on the bread and then the onion-apple mix from the pan.

8. Now enjoy. **Æbleflæsk** tastes better while still warm.

27. Technology

Nowadays, everything is digital, so let us go digital with some words related to our digital lives or our workspaces.

#	Danish	English
481	computer	computer
482	bærbare computer	laptop
483	internettet	the Internet
484	smartphone	smartphone
485	at søge (på internettet)	to search (the internet)
486	to call	to call
487	tastatur	keyboard
488	mus	mouse
489	kamera	camera
490	hovedtelefoner	headphones

28. The last 10 words

And now get ready for the final ten words before you reach the 500 Danish words. Here I want to present you ten words that might not be the most useful ones in everyday life, but some beautiful and inspiring words that hopefully will motivate you even more to continue learning Danish.

#	Danish	English
491	tillykke	congratulations
492	viden	knowledge
493	horisont	horizon
494	solnedgang	sunset
495	nordlys	aurora

And the last five ones on the next page are very special and somewhat exclusive to Danish

496 Arbejdsglæde

In Denmark, you say you are **arbejdsglæde** if you have happiness at work or high job satisfaction. This is an important aspect for many Danes and a part of the work culture in this country.

497 Overmorgen

In English we simply call the day after tomorrow *the day after tomorrow*, but in the Danish language there is a word for that. With **overmorgen** you can express this in a quicker and easier way. The literal translation would mean something like "over tomorrow" in English. And as a small extra: **Forgårs** means *the day before yesterday*.

498 Velbekomme

You remember the Æbleflæsk recipe? If yes, and you actually went to cook and try it for yourself I should have told you **velbekomme** before you enjoyed it. This word translates to something like enjoy your meal or bon appétit (for the French speakers here).

499 Forelsket

Danes use **forelsket** if they are madly in love with somebody, the word is much stronger than just being in love and describes the intense feeling and euphoria of falling or being in love. Maybe those last words you learn today will lead you to falling in love with the Danish language even more.

500 Hygge

When you read about Denmark you probably read about **hygge** a thousand times, and it is really an important part of the Danish lifestyle. **Hygge** is about a cozy, warm and relaxed atmosphere especially in the cold months of the year. When everything is cold and dark outside, Danes like to sit at home with their family and friends, maybe drink a warm tea and sit in front of a fireplace or play board games or just watch an entertaining movie while the candlelight flickers on the windowsill. Really every Dane has an own interpretation of **hygge**, but the main concept of coziness is always the same.

29. Extra: the longest Danish word

And wait, I have another word for you, one you will probably never use, and you should not even try to remember, because it is the longest Danish word. With 51 letters it is truly long and got the entry as the longest Danish word in the Danish version of the Guinness Book of World Records in 1993. It should be noted that the word does not really make a lot of sense and that there are indications that it was never used in a book with its real meaning, except for citations as it being the longest Danish word.

And here is the word:

Speciallægepraksisplanlægningsstabilliseringsperiode

The meaning is really interesting and very useful (irony) because **speciallægepraksisplanlægningsstabiliseringsperiode** translated means:

a period of stabilizing the planning of a specialist doctor's practice

I hope you enjoyed this small bonus word.

30. Test your Danish skills

I hope you had some fun learning Danish, but now it is time to use some of that skill you gained during the last weeks. Below you will find a short text in Danish you should be able to understand with your level now. The text is almost exclusively using vocabulary you learned on the pages before.

30.1 My way home

Jeg har min bagage i hånden og går indenfor på hovedbanegården, togene ankommer og afgår. Jeg kan se, at mit tog er forsinket. På min billet er afgangstiden 10:30, men toget kommer 30 minutter for sent.

Toget ankommer, og jeg sætter mig på min plads. Det er et vinduessæde med nummer 39. Jeg tager min bærbare computer frem og ser en bevægelse. Toget ankommer til Aalborg, en lille by i Danmark. Der er ingen taxa, så jeg går til fods til det hus, jeg ejer. På min vej ser jeg en butik, den hedder Netto og jeg går ind for at købe en flaske vand og brød. Jeg går til kassen, og personen ved kassen spørger mig, om jeg betaler kontant eller med kort. Jeg betaler med kort, det er 28 kroner, hun giver mig kvitteringen og jeg går udenfor og går ind i en bus.

Jeg kommer hjem foran døren. Jeg kommer ind og tænder lyset i gangen og går ud i køkkenet. Jeg åbner køleskabet og tager noget ost, som jeg putter på brødet. Jeg sætter mig ved bordet i stuen og spiser ostebrødet. På fjernsynet ser jeg en film om restauranter i Danmark. Den siger, at der er en tendens til mere vegetarisk og vegansk mad, og folk køber flere grøntsager som avocado eller kartofler. Jeg er færdig med mit brød og går på toilettet og går i bad, efter dette børster jeg tænder med tandbørsten. Jeg går ind i soveværelset og lægger mig inde i min seng og sover. Godnat.

31. Some facts about Denmark

Flag fact:

Denmark has the oldest state flag in the world. The Dannebrog, how the flag is commonly called, holds the world record for the oldest national flag in continues use. First uses of the flag date back to the year 1219 while the official adoption of the flag as a national flag happened in 1625. Danes love their flag, and you will see many of them on birthday parties.

Fact vocabulary: national flag → national flag

Mountain fact:

Denmark is really flat. There are no real mountains, only hills and the highest elevation is about 170 meters or 558 feet above sea level. But taking a look at the other Danish territories we find a real mountain called Gunnbjørn on Greenland that is about 3700 meters or 12139 feet tall.

Fact vocabulary: mountain → bjerg

Territory fact:

Well, *fact 2* already hinted at this, but Denmark is not only Denmark, the Kingdom of Denmark, also called the Danish Realm, consists of the piece of land that lies just north of Germany plus two other territories that include the Faroe Islands and Greenland. Both are self-governed and have autonomous legal systems. While Denmark for example is part of the European Union, Greenland is not an official member, but it is a part of *the overseas countries and territories* of a member state and thus its citizens are also EU citizens with the right to move and reside freely within the EU.

Fact vocabulary: territory → territorium

Border fact:

Denmark only has one direct land border with another country. The only neighboring country that Denmark has a land border with is Germany. And the border is about 68 kilometers or 42 miles long. But this fact will need a revision in the future since Denmark will very likely gain another direct land border with a very unlikely country. This country is Canada, a country that for now also only has one border with another country. The story behind this is quite interesting and plays around *Hans Island*, a small uninhabited piece of rock in the arctic region with an area of 1.3 square kilometers or 0.50 square miles. Canada and Denmark had a territorial dispute over Hans Island for a long time but settled for a split of the island after 17 years of negotiations in 2022. As the ratification of the laws is still outstanding it is not official at the time of writing, but would result in the creation of a new border between Canada and Denmark.

Fact vocabulary: border → grænse

Island fact:

While talking about islands, let us talk about the number of islands that belong to Denmark. That would be 406 (not including the Faroe Islands or Greenland) and the far majority of about 336 is uninhabited. Since only one person living there means that they have a population, this number is subject to change regularly. The three biggest islands are Zealand, North Jutlandic Island and Funen.

Fact vocabulary: island → ø

Sea fact:

You are never more than 50 kilometers or 31 miles away from the sea in Denmark. The country is almost completely surrounded by water from all directions.

Fact vocabulary: sea → hav

Viking fact:

Denmark was the home of the Vikings and at one point the Viking empire stretched from Denmark to Norway, parts of Sweden, Greenland, the Faroe Island plus parts of the British Isles. With their brilliant navigation skills, they travelled to places like North America, Russia and Turkey, mainly for plundering or trade. The Vikings spoke a form of Danish called the *dǫnsk tunga* today translated as *Old Norse*.

Fact vocabulary: Vikings → Vikinger

King fact:

Do you still remember Bluetooth? This wireless technology standard is actually named after the Danish King Harald Bluetooth who ruled the Denmark and Norway from 958 – 986. The Bluetooth logo is actually a combination of his initials H. and B. from the Scandinavian rune system. The respective runes are the *Younger Futhark* ᛘ and the *Bind rune* ᛒ.

Fact vocabulary: king → konge

Language fact:

Danish, like other Germanic languages used to distinct between a formal and a personal way of saying *you*. This distinction is gone and only the regular **du** is used, but if you want to be super old-fashioned and formal you can use **de**, I wonder though if Danes will appreciate this form.

Fact vocabulary: language → sprog

32. Understanding the news

OK I know, the book promised only 500 Words, but sometimes it is difficult to choose the words that are most relevant in your specific context. Since one learning strategy can be to learn some basic words and then improve the understanding of the language by reading news articles and watching movies in Danish I now present you with the 100 most common words in Danish news articles of the recent weeks at the time of writing this guide. For this data set I analyzed articles from various Danish news outlets and cleaned up the basic connectors, personal pronouns and more to have a proper set of "news words" used in Danish reporting, so that you can understand those articles more easily.

#	Danish	English
1	seneste	most recent
2	som	as
3	fra	from
4	ikke	does not
5	skal	shall
6	ved	by
7	sig	themselves
8	efter	after
9	siger	say
10	vil	will
11	blev	became
12	mod	against
13	kan	able to
14	Ukraine	Ukraine
15	dag	day
16	men	but
17	var	was
18	ret	right
19	over	over
20	hjem	home

#	Danish	English
21	alle	all
22	flere	more
23	butikker	shops
24	nye	new
25	sigtet	charged
26	Foto	Photo
27	bliver	becomes
28	ogs	also
29	lande	countries
30	Danmark	Denmark
31	lige	just
32	blandt	among
33	andet	other things
34	under	below
35	paa	on
36	igen	again
37	meget	much
38	embedsm	official
39	gang	walk
40	mere	more
41	mange	many
42	andre	others
43	mellem	between
44	viser	shows
45	tidligere	earlier
46	tale	talk
47	skulle	should
48	ende	end
49	millioner	millions
50	tog	train
51	dage	days
52	tage	take
53	imod	against
54	region	region
55	derfor	Therefore

#	Danish	English
56	fort	fast
57	nogle	some
58	komme	come
59	mener	means
60	uger	weeks
61	oplyser	informs
62	cirka	about
63	ber	pray
64	optagelsespr	admission
65	omkring	around
66	Rusland	Russia
67	krav	requirements
68	fik	got
69	milliarder	billions
70	ekstra	additional
71	passagerer	passengers
72	gennem	through
73	siden	since
74	eller	or
75	danskerne	the Danes
76	slutningen	the end
77	medier	media
78	hackerangreb	hacker attack
79	varet	lasted
80	ser	looking
81	hos	with
82	anholdt	arrested
83	begynder	begins
84	sende	send
85	blok	block
86	samme	same
87	kritik	criticism
88	videre	continue
89	sidste	last
90	eftermiddag	afternoon

#	Danish	English
91	sporten	the sport
92	ben	leg
93	donorkonference	donor conference
94	sammen	together
95	vejret	weather
96	direkt	directly
97	vaccination	vaccination
98	kun	only
99	bne	bone
100	lyder	sounds

33. List of Danish online newspapers

As Danish is not spoken by many people around the world, the number of newspapers and news sources in Danish is very limited and often focused on local and regional news. But there is also a number of bigger players in the market that cover the whole of Denmark plus world news.

Below you find a selection of news sources that you can choose from to improve your Danish skills. But practise is needed to understand whole articles, the aim here should be to get used to Danish writing and get information from context. Happy reading!

Newspaper	Description	Web
DR	Danish public-service broadcasting company	dr.dk
Politiken	Politics focused	politiken.dk
Ekstra Bladet	Tabloid newspaper	ekstrabladet.dk
Berlingske	Daily national newspaper; among the oldest newspapers in the world	berlingske.dk
Jyllands-Posten	Tabloid newspaper	jyllands-posten.dk
BT	General news	bt.dk
TV2 News	Government-run television station	nyheder.tv2.dk

34. The End

That is it, the end of this Danish guide in 500 words. I hope you enjoyed the learning and the small fun facts and are still motivated to continue your path of learning Danish. Because 500 words is just a good beginning, with room for further improvement. It is beautiful to learn a new language and extremely fun if you reach a level where you can actually use the learned words. So I want to wish you all the best for your further journey.

Held og lykke!

Best regards from Aalborg, Denmark.

Printed in Great Britain
by Amazon

54564426R00046